# CRYPTOCURRENCY

The Essential Guide to understanding Bitcoin, Blockchain and More

By

Devan Hansel

Copyright © 2017

All rights reserved. No part of this book may be reproduced or transmitted in any form or by any means, electronic or mechanical, including photocopying, recording or by any information storage and retrieval system without written permission of the publisher, except for the inclusion of brief quotations in a review.

# Disclaimer

No part of this publication may be reproduced or transmitted in any form or by any means, mechanical or electronic, including photocopying or recording, or by any information storage and retrieval system, or transmitted by email without permission in writing from the publisher.

While all attempts have been made to verify the information provided in this publication, neither the author nor the publisher assumes any responsibility for errors, omissions, or contrary interpretations of the subject matter herein.

This book is for entertainment purposes only. The views expressed are those of the author alone, and should not be taken as expert instruction or commands. The reader is responsible for his or her own actions.

Adherence to all applicable laws and regulations, including international, federal, state, and local governing professional licensing, business practices, advertising, and all other aspects of doing business in the US, Canada, or any other jurisdiction is the sole responsibility of the purchaser or reader.

Neither the author nor the publisher assumes any responsibility or liability whatsoever on the behalf of the purchaser or reader of these materials.

Any perceived slight of any individual or organization is purely unintentional

# Note to the Readers

Research studies have shown that 42% of people never read another book after graduating from college. So I'd like to commend you for actually following up on your curiosity by getting this book. Given the public interest and rising market valuation of cryptocurrencies, this book is expectedly a smart and timely purchase. The value of cryptocurrencies has skyrocketed since their inception back in 2009 with Bitcoin. A window of opportunity has opened up for those who are interested enough to learn and brave enough to invest. Make no mistake, there is a lot of wealth to be made in this field. 5 years from now, people will look back and wonder why they didn't get on the boat while they still had the chance. The fact that you've bought this book indicates your interest. But are you willing to seize the opportunity? If you really are, I suggest you read the next section titled "Get the FREE Bonus".

A lot of time and effort has gone into creating the book you are now reading. And I sincerely hope that it helps you move ahead in your quest for knowledge. The book has been designed to take you gradually through the hoops and introduce the cryptocurrency landscape, one block at a time. As such, care has been taken to ensure that anybody can read and understand the material without too many prerequisites. The book has also been written in a short-and-concise format so as to allow readers to go through the book quickly.

However, if you happen to find it difficult at times, please go through the resources recommended within the context. I hope you have a good time reading the book :)

## Get the FREE Bonus

If you're interested in receiving free PDFs on latest strategies and tips about stuff like cryptocurrency, online trading, investing, real estate, stock market etc, I highly recommend you to join my list (link below) where members get to learn how to make money and invest it wisely. As a bonus, you will also be getting my latest books for FREE before anyone else. It's an exclusive list and the link to join can be found below. It doesn't cost you anything to join. You will only have to put in your email-id so that I can connect with you and keep you updated. It's a clear win-win. So go ahead and subscribe now.

http://bit.ly/devan-hansel

# About the Author

Hi there! I am Devan Hansel. I live in the States with my dog, Milo. Over the years, I've acquired a wide range of experiences in investing and the art of money-making by getting involved in the stock market, real estate, startups and more recently...cryptocurrencies. Having a technology background, I could easily grasp the essence of it and understand how the whole system works. And in this book, I will lay it all out before you. As far as my track record goes, I've successfully invested in cryptocurrencies like bit coin (BTC), ethereal (ETH), dash (DASH) and many others (you will learn about these in the chapters ahead). Although it takes careful planning to develop an investment strategy and follow it through, the profits and the rush you get from making a successful trade are definitely worth it.

My intention in writing this book is to share the basic knowledge of cryptocurrency that you need, along with some investment tips and tactics. The cryptocurrency market is in a very early stage(less than 8 years old) and there are huge profits to be made. Venture Capitalists have invested billions of dollars to make this technology work. Millionaires have been made in this market. And the exciting part is that you can make a lot of profit and also fund groundbreaking technology at the same time. It's like hitting two birds with the same stone. As the saying goes, the best time to start is now.

I have personally benefited a lot from having spent time and money in this field. And in this book, I've shared all the essential knowledge that you need to get started on your own journey. Good luck!

# Table of Contents

CHAPTER 1: WHAT ACTUALLY IS CURRENCY? ........................................................ 1

CHAPTER 2: EMERGENCE OF CRYPTOCURRENCY ................................................ 11

CHAPTER 3: SO HOW DOES IT ALL WORK? ......................................................... 25

CHAPTER 4: INVESTING IN CRYPTOCURRENCIES ................................................. 55

CHAPTER 5: FUTURE OF CRYPTOCURRENCY ....................................................... 67

CHAPTER 6: CONCLUSION ................................................................................. 74

# Chapter 1

## What actually is Currency?

*Brief overview of money and digital currency*

A Before we dive into the nitty-gritty details of cryptocurrencies and the technology that drives them, it is important to understand some essential concepts of money to appreciate the evolution of this system over time. It will also help us understand why cryptocurrencies actually hold value which is something that most beginners can get confused with. So let's begin.

**What is Money?**
Money can be defined broadly as a form of physical/virtual representation of value that is recognized by the participating entities in a transaction. While transacting, people need a measurement of value and that's basically where money comes in. Money has certain general properties like public acceptability, stability of value, portability etc.

Currency is the set of all individual units of money (like bank notes, coins) that are in use at any given time. The measurement and representation of value varies across countries. Hence we have different currencies (e.g., Dollar (USD) in America, Pound (GBP) in United Kingdom, Baht (THB) in Thailand, and Rupee (INR) in India). A good currency has certain properties like scarcity, divisibility, transferability.

**Note**: In addition to the different currencies, the value of a substance (good or service) itself can also vary across countries. This is the basis for *bureau de change* and *forex* (foreign exchange) trading which are business and trading mechanisms that operate primarily by exchanging currencies. For example, you can sell a product in Dollars (USD) and get paid in Pounds (GBP). You will make profit/loss depending on the value-difference of the product, as measured by the two currencies. For currency trends and access to currency conversion tools, you can check out the resources at the following URL.

https://www.oanda.com/currency/converter/

**Money vs. Currency**

Although money and currency are used interchangeably in most circumstances, they are not exactly the same. Here are the general differences.

| *Money* | *Currency* |
|---|---|
| 1. Money is a medium of exchange. It is used to measure and represent value. | 1. Currency is a system of monetary units. It represents money in physical/virtual form. |
| 2. It is an abstract concept. There is nothing tangible about it. | 2. Currency is real and tangible. It is the dollar bills and coins that you can touch and feel with your hands. |
| 3. The amount of total money is fixed. Like the amount of gold in the world. | 3. Currency can be created by printing notes or minting coins. |

| | |
|---|---|
| 4. Money is highly durable and persists for a very long time. | 4. Currencies can rise and fall, as society progresses. They can be wiped out totally. |
| 5. Money can exist without currency. | 5. Currency does not exist without money. |

**The Origin of Money**

Around 100,000 years back there was nothing much going on, in regards to social and economic development of humanity. As we got better at survival, gathering food, building tribes, we started to progress. Eventually we were able to grow our own food, build all kinds of tools and offer services to each other. At this point, we had no way of calculating the value of our goods and services. We could estimate the perceived value but there was no system or standard as such. So we just exchanged them directly. For example, one apple for two bananas, three bags of rice for a knife etc. This is called the Barter system. It is a way of exchanging goods and services where there is no standard way of calculating value.

As trade & commerce took off, people developed various pricing standards to exchange goods. For example, tobacco was the common unit of exchange in Virginia while beaver pelts were more common in Canada. Further down the timeline, we started mining metals and trading with gold and silver. This is where the concept of *Commodity money* came into existence. It is a form of value represented intrinsically by the commodities themselves.

The merchants who exchanged gold for other commodities also issued receipts as a guarantee so that buyers can exchange the gold to get their commodities back. These receipts of paper slowly garnered acceptance among traders and the general public. They represented trust and value because one could always exchange them for gold. This was when the concept of *paper money* came into the picture. The first paper money created by a bank was introduced in China by the Tang & Song dynasties in $7^{th}$ century A.D.

**Gold Standard**

While paper money started getting popular in Europe, people were still using coins for buying and selling stuff up till 17th century. To discourage people from using gold directly and use paper notes instead, a monetary system called the gold standard was put in place. Paper notes issued by the government were equated with appropriate fixed amount of gold. For example, 100 notes would have the same value as 1 gram of gold. And this was bound in law and protected by the government so that people could trade and exchange value with notes instead of gold.

The British West Indies (now divided into separate countries) was one of the first provinces to adopt a gold standard. In 1717, Sir Isaac Newton who was the master of the *Royal Mint* set a new silver-to-gold mint ratio and this drove out silver from the circulated currency and established a gold standard for Britain.

Although many countries still hold gold reserves, the system of gold standard has been abandoned. The U.S government led by President Nixon gave up the gold standard in 1971 which means that you can no longer uphold the government (and private banks) to exchange dollars for equivalent amount of gold. Since 1971, the U.S has been using a fiat currency system for representing its money.

**Fiat Currency**

In economics, fiat money is defined as: "...an intrinsically valueless object or record that is widely accepted as money."

Fiat money is what most people think money is. It consists of the paper-notes and metal-coins that a government declares as money by issuing a legal tender. But unlike the gold standard, the value of fiat money is not dependent on external factors like the amount of gold available. It is pure value as upheld by the government without any attachment or constraint. So the government doesn't have to exchange your fiat money with, for example, an equivalent amount of gold.

## 10 interesting facts about money & currency

- The oldest minted coin known has the face of a roaring lion on it.
- The first human face to appear on a coin was that of Julius Caesar in 44 B.C.
- The world *"money"* comes from *"Moneta"* which is the name of the goddess in whose temple coins were made in ancient Rome.
- There are over 170 different currencies in use currently in the world.
- During World War 2, Germany snuck in a lot of fake bills into England to dilute its currency and break their financial system. America did the same with Japan.
- The U.S Dollar was first recognized in 1785. It is currently the most traded currency around the world.
- Only 5% of global money is cash. The rest is digital.
- According to estimates, the U.S government prints around $974 million every year to replace old and worn out dollar bills.
- 94% of paper money is contaminated with bacteria. Yikes!

- The most counterfeited bill of all time is the $100 bill.

## Digital Currency

Money dealt with using electronic systems is digital currency. This kind of money is called *virtual money* or *cybercash*. Every unit of virtual money can be mapped to a memory block in some digital storage device like a hard disk. It is essentially stored and transferred over the internet using network servers and databases. There are many advantages to this type of transactions. For instance, unlike physical transfer of cash which can be a hassle sometimes (risky, time-consuming, transaction fee etc), digital transactions over the internet can not only be safe but also instantaneous provided the right software is used.

There are multiple forms of digital currency.

**Virtual Currency** is a digital representation of money which is purely online i.e, it does not have a physical counterpart. It essentially consists of virtual assets (called digital money) that are not regulated by a central financial authority. So the reach and usage is limited to specific online communities that accept it.

**Cryptocurrency** is a digital currency in which the money is stored, transferred and verified using cryptographic techniques. It is also a virtual currency. So the individual monetary units of the cryptocurrency (e.g, bitcoins) are created and safeguarded using complex encryption/decryption algorithms. Many cryptocurrency systems are decentralized i.e, they are not controlled by a central bank or government authority. We will look into the effectiveness of cryptocurrencies in further chapters.

# Chapter 2

## Emergence of Cryptocurrency

*What is it and how did it come to be?*

As we've already seen in the previous chapter, cryptocurrency is just a digital currency in which cryptographic techniques are used for

(i) generating the individual units of currency

(ii) transfer and verification of those units between holders

Before we proceed with learning more about cryptocurrency, it is important to get an understanding of basic cryptography terminology. If you are already familiar with these concepts, you can skip to the next section (although a quick brush-up of fundamental wouldn't hurt). But if you're not, it is suggested that you go through the following section at your own pace. It covers the basic concepts of cryptography in the context of cryptocurrencies. This is necessary for proceeding with further chapters.

## Brief Overview of Cryptography

Cryptography is just a way of dealing with secrets and codes that are designed to conceal the underlying data (like messages) for safety reasons. So anything from morse code to advanced computer algorithms falls under the field of cryptography.

**Encryption**: The process of converting a message into a code that is not readable by unauthorized entities.

**Decryption**: It's just the opposite of encryption i.e, the process of converting an encrypted code into it's corresponding message.

**Cipher & Key**: A cipher is an algorithm (sequence of steps) that can perform encryption or decryption on data. It uses a supplementary element called the *key* which feeds into the algorithm to generate unique encryptions. It is impossible to decrypt a code generated by a cipher without its key.

**Hash function**: These are mathematical operations that convert data of any size to a fixed-length output. They have widespread usage in various fields of computer science.

**Cryptographic Hash Function**: A cryptographic hash function is a special kind of hash function which is identified by three properties:

(i) Given an input, calculating the output of the function is very easy.

(ii) Given an output, calculating its input for the function is extremely hard. In fact, it is considered computationally impossible.

(iii) The probability of two similar inputs having the same output for the function is extremely low.

**SHA**: Designed by the N.S.A and short for Secure Hash Algorithm, it is a cryptographic hash function that contains a set of encryption functions. SHA256 converts input data to a "hash" output value which can then be communicated openly without worry of someone figuring out the input. The beauty of SHA is that it is easy to verify it's output but hard to calculate its input. So it is essentially a one-way lock. SHA-256 is a famous hash function and it converts data into 256-bit sized hash outputs. It is used in almost all the online security frameworks.

**Public & Private Key**: This is a form of communication where two parties can communicate (send & receive messages) between each other without having any third party interfere or disrupt their communication. The method involves two parties (let's say Alice and Bob) who want to communicate securely with each other. Each of the parties has a pair of cryptographic keys out of which one is public and one is private. Everybody knows everyone else's public key but nobody knows anyone else's private key. The math behind this pair of keys works such that when a message is encrypted with Alice's private key, it can only be decrypted using Alice's public key and vice versa.

So the idea is that when Alice wants to send a secret message directed at Bob, she will encrypt the message with her private key and Bob's public key. When Bob receives the encrypted message, he will decrypt it with Alice's public key and his own private key.

**Digital Signature**: When communicating over an insecure channel, it helps to have a way of verifying the identity of people involved. A digital signature helps to do just that. They are usually contained as certificates or implied through ciphers. For example, the private key of Alice can serve as her digital signature of sorts because encrypting a message using it will confirm to the receiver (who decrypts using public key of Alice) that it is Alice on the other side and not someone else.

With this understanding, we can proceed further with cryptocurrencies and how/why they work. Don't worry too much if you're overwhelmed by all the technical definitions above. You can come back and refer to this section if you're unsure in the future. But to get a better picture, let's start with how all of this got started in the first place.

**The Origin of Cryptocurrency**

Throughout history, we've been using different mediums of exchange like commodity money, paper money, gold standard, fiat currencies etc. But over the years, different communities (especially scientific) across the world had been dissatisfied with the short-comings of these traditional currencies. Due to the explosion of internet and progress made in the fields of cryptography, online security, digital payments, it became possible to have a totally decentralized currency that could void the necessity of a central bank or government.

After the 9/11 attacks, America got very strict on the digital front. Laws like the *Patriot Act* were passed to perform online surveillance at a mass level. Needless to say, cryptocurrencies were shunned down owing to their decentralized structure and assumed to be hotbeds for terrorists and other illegal activists.

The first sign of cryptocurrency came when an American cryptographer named David Chaum founded the company *DigiCash* in Netherlands (since it was likely to get shut down in America). DigiCash used *blinding algorithms* to protect user's money and transaction details. However, they had complete monopoly over the supply of the currency and they dealt with the users directly. This made the Central Bank of Netherlands call foul which meant that DigiCash would have to either sell the company or shut it down soon. Although Microsoft approached DigiCash with an offer of $180 million, Chaum thought that it was not enough. So Microsoft took the offer off the table and DigiCash ran out of funds eventually.

Shortly after that, many cryptocurrency systems like *b-money* and *BitGold* came into light but never took off. They had all the necessary components like blockchain systems, anonymity protection, decentralization etc but somehow couldn't get enough attention in the marketplace for widespread usage.

The first modern cryptocurrency to emerge that is effective and used widely is Bitcoin. A white-paper explaining the details of bitcoin implementation was first published under the pseudo-name of *Satoshi Nakamoto* in October 2008. The paper is titled *"Bitcoin : A Peer-to-Peer Electronic Cash System"* and can be downloaded at **www.bitcoin.org/bitcoin.pdf**. On January 2009, Satoshi released the initial version of the bitcoin software on SourceForge.net, opening the technology up to the public. To this day, the real identity of Satoshi Nakomoto remains a mystery. Based on bitcoin transaction logs, it is estimated that Satoshi owns roughly 1 million bitcoins which are currently evaluated at 2.8 billion dollars!

Cryptocurrencies are slowly being accepted by all major companies and startups, especially in Silicon Valley. WordPress became the first major company to accept bitcoins in 2012. Soon after, big shots like Microsoft, Dell, Virgin Group, Lamborghini followed. Currently, the total market cap for all cryptocurrencies has exceeded $100 billion. This is an indication that the world is slowly shifting towards decentralized cryptocurrencies for a myriad of reasons.

**Different types of cryptocurrencies**

More than 900 public cryptocurrencies exist in the world and many more are created every month. In this section, we will look at the most prominent cryptocurrencies. To view the updated trends and market capitalizations of the top 100 cryptocurrencies, check out **www.coinmarketcap.com**.

1. **Bitcoin (BTC):** This is the first known cryptocurrency to be well-recognized and used by the public. It has paved the way for modern cryptocurrencies and is considered the de facto standard. Almost all the other cryptocurrencies have either

branched off from or have major commonalities with bitcoin. Market cap of bitcoin is around 46 billion dollars currently making it the largest publicly traded digital currency. At the time of this writing, one bitcoin is worth $2493.

2. **Litecoin (LTC)**: Launched around 2 years after bitcoin, litecoin is a decentralized peer-to-peer cryptocurrency with a growing network of developers, merchants and supporters. Although very similar to bitcoin, it offers relatively faster transaction confirmations. As of May 2017, the market cap of litecoin is around 1.5 billion dollars. Where bitcoin is gold, litecoin is silver. One litecoin is worth $31 during the time of this writing.

3. **Ethereum(ETH)** : Launched recently(2015), ethereum is also a decentralized cryptocurrency but offers more functionality like *smart contracts*, the *ethereum virtual machine*, distributed computing etc. Currently, ethereum is the second largest cryptocurrency with a market cap of 24 billion dollars. As of the time of this writing, one *ether* unit is worth $362.

4. **Ripple (XRP)**: Ripple is heavily used by banks to settle global transactions in a secure and effective way at very low costs. It is different from bitcoin in its protocol and structure. Unlike bitcoin, ripple doesn't require high computing power for creation of new currency. As a result, it has a reduced network latency. The individual units of Ripple currency are called *ripples* (XRP). One ripple is worth $0.26 and the overall currency has a market capitalization of 11 billion dollars making it the third largest cryptocurrency.

5. **Dash (DASH)**: Originally known as DarkCoin, Dash is also a decentralized peer-to-peer cryptocurrency like Bitcoin albeit a more secretive one. It was launched in January 2014 and experienced a surge in traffic and fan-following quickly. Its famous features include instant transactions (*InstantSend*) and complete private transactions (*PrivateSend*). It also uses a separate chained hashing algorithm called X11 unlike bitcoin's SHA256. Market cap for Dash is around 1 billion dollars and one Dash coin will cost you $165 (at of time of this writing).

*Note*: Cryptocurrencies other than Bitcoin are referred to as "Altcoins" because they are alternatives launched after Bitcoin.

## Bitcoin

As you must've already understood by now, the most promising and widely used cryptocurrency is bitcoin. So let's look at exactly what makes bitcoin such an awesome currency and why it's a no-brainer to invest in bitcoin. For a deep-dive into bitcoin and how you can potentially make thousands of dollars mining and trading bitcoins, I'd recommend you to check out my book *"Bitcoin: The Digital Gold"* on amazon. It will give you some insights into the technology and how to proceed with getting involved in it.

### Why Bitcoin is a good currency

1. **Scarcity**: Only 21 million bitcoins can ever exist. We will see why in further chapters. This cap on the total amount of bitcoins ensures that its net value never drops too low. As the economy grows, the value of bitcoin also increases. It is estimated that one bitcoin will be worth around 1 million dollars in less than 20

years. And it costs less than 3000 dollars at the time of this writing. (If you're planning to purchase and invest in bitcoins, check out Chapter-5)

2. **Durability**: The whole purpose of currency is to represent money in a physical/virtual form so that people can have easier time exchanging value. If the currency fades away with time or gets worn out over repeated use, it can be a hassle to keep churning out more currency to replace the damage. All physical currencies are prone to physical damage like wear & tear, weather etc. This is where bitcoin trumps all other forms of currencies because it is 100% digital. The life-time of a bitcoin is theoretically infinite. It will survive as long as there's an operating network that runs the bitcoin protocol. A decentralized network, high level of encryption, digitized currency and the existential guarantee of internet in the foreseeable future make bitcoin one of the most durable currencies ever created.

3. **Interchangeable**: We already know that currency is just a set of monetary units in use. As such, a good currency is one in which the units are interchangeable. This means that all the units should be identical in *structure* and represent the same amount of value. Take gold for example. 1 gram of gold has the same value anywhere. Similarly, 1 bitcoin is exactly the same as the other. For all practical purposes, you can exchange 1 bitcoin with another and there would be no difference in value.

4. **Divisibility**: To measure and grade value, a good currency needs to be divisible to the smallest required scale (e.g, dollars & cents, pounds & sterlings, rupees & paisa). The bitcoin protocol has been designed in such a way that you can divide one bitcoin into many smaller units called Satoshis which can be further divided if necessary.

5. **Transferability**: If you have a working internet connection and a computer (smartphone or tablet will also work), you can transfer bitcoins with just a couple of clicks. This makes it a very convenient mode of money transfer unlike bank cheques and

wire transfers. There is no central authority or third party that charges a transfer fee so it is also a more profitable mode of money transfer.

# Chapter 3

## So how does it all work?

### *The Cryptocurrency Eco-system*

In this chapter, we will look at the basic guidelines which every cryptocurrency operates with. As it happens, there are many different versions available in the market and it helps to know the fundamental framework that all of them are based on. If you're a beginner to this technology, make sure to take your time while going through the different sections. Reference links have been provided where necessary for better understanding.

**What is Blockchain?**
Let us begin by asking the question – what do we need a currency for? We need currency so that we can give it to others (buying) or take it from others (selling). Isn't this right? And for a cryptocurrency, that is where a blockchain comes into the picture. Blockchain is a technology that allows people to transfer

cryptocurrency between one another securely. It is a distributed database where all the transaction records are saved. Unlike a typical fiat currency, the blockchain of cryptocurrency is distributed and spread across various countries and individuals. The databases and servers are run by volunteers who maintain a peer-to-peer network. There is no possibility of government or any third-party involvement in manipulating the database records. Even if the government officials or any malicious entities volunteer for maintaining the blockchain, they cannot alter the transaction records due to the constraints imposed by its design.

Blockchain is essentially an open electronic ledger where all transactions are recorded for public viewing. For example, the latest bitcoin transactions can be found at: **https://blockchain.info/**. This open strategy of blockchain prevents counterfeits and other frauds. By checking the blockchain, you can be sure that the transactions are completely legitimate. Once you make a transaction, it will appear shortly in the public blockchain.

You might be wondering, *"But won't people know who's spending how much by looking at the blockchain?"* The answer to that is *No* because your identity is protected using encryption and mapping functions. Only your Wallet-ID will appear in the blockchain which reveals nothing about your personal identity. We will cover the mechanics of a cryptocurrency wallet later in this chapter.

**What is Mining?**

Now that we have an idea of what the blockchain is, it is necessary to understand how it is updated unanimously throughout the network. It has to be unanimous because if the status of blockchain is not congruent among the nodes, it will lead to discrepancies in verifying transactions which will result in frauds and eventual system failure. So let's look into this in detail.

There are two kinds of nodes in a blockchain network. Normal nodes and mining nodes. Both of these have their own separate operating protocols. And every node maintains its own blockchain, constructed individually by adding valid blocks to the list. The normal nodes have relatively basic functionality. They receive transaction-messages from neighboring nodes in the network and their job is to verify the transactions and propagate them forward to remaining nodes. This will ensure that as time goes by, only verified transactions are spread across the network. This is a basic layer of security to ensure bogus transactions are not updated in the blockchain.

Now, the mining nodes are a different kind of nodes that execute the mining protocol which includes the following steps.

- Listen for new transactions and verify them.
- Aggregate verified transactions into a block.
- Compute the solution to an algorithm called *Proof-of-Work* for that specific block.
- Timestamp the block along with the computed *proof-of-work* and broadcast it across the network.

The mining nodes essentially group new valid transactions into blocks and propagate them to other nodes. The validity of the block can be measured by any node by checking the *proof-of-work* value. So when this new block is received by the remaining nodes, they check its validity and add it to their own blockchain. A reward is given to the mining node that propagated the valid block with the earliest timestamp. This reward is usually a certain amount of cryptocurrency units. It is similar to the processing fee charged by banks and other financial organizations.

Now we know how blocks are mined, how the blockchain is built and how the *Proof-of-Work* protocol helps in making sure that every node on the network is on the same page when it comes to the blockchain. Here's the interesting bit. In most cryptocurrencies (including Bitcoin), mining is the only way to create new crypto-coins. That is to say, the only way for the system to assign value to the cryptocurrency is to measure the amount of computation performed by the mining nodes. Every bitcoin ever "minted" has been the result of a mining node performing the *Proof-of-Work* algorithm to create a new valid block.

So the purpose of mining is two fold. To create new cryptocurrency and update the blockchain with valid transactions. The reason that miners are rewarded is to incentivize them to perform the needed computation. If there was no reward, there wouldn't be enough miners to validate the transactions quickly. This would lead to a relatively unsafe system due to its high latency. The security of the cryptocurrency depends on how fast the transactions are verified. And that depends on how many miners are competing for the reward simultaneously. This is the beauty of the bitcoin-blockchain system design. And also, the reward for mining goes down by 50% every 4 years for the bitcoin system. Eventually, there would be no reward for mining blocks except for the transaction fee and tips. This is a way to ensure that the value of the cryptocurrency doesn't go down below a certain point because of limited supply.

The Blockchain is the heart of most cryptocurrencies. It is the bedrock on which all the transactions, security and efficiency of the system rely upon. Moreover, the tech community across the globe is waking up to the ingenuity of the blockchain design. Numerous applications of the blockchain technology are being identified in all areas of the digital spectrum. It may as well be that we've stumbled upon the backbone of a new kind of internet. If you're really interested in learning more about this to get a complete perspective, I'd recommend you to check out my book *"Blockchain: The Technology Revolution behind Bitcoin and Cryptocurrency"*. It covers everything you need to understand how the technology works, how it fits in with cryptocurrencies and why people are so hyped about it.

The two main problems that a blockchain solves are:
1. Decentralized Consensus
2. Double Spending

## How Decentralized Consensus Works

The architecture of the blockchain is such that it eliminates the need for a central database or monitoring authority. You have to understand that this is a groundbreaking technological revolution not only in the field of digital currency but also in business, banking, governance, politics etc. A plethora of possibilities have opened up after it has been proven that a system like bitcoin can be developed which achieves decentralized consensus in a secure and efficient manner. New self-verifying systems and decentralized apps are being developed today on account of this innovation.

To those who are unaware, decentralized consensus is when a network of entities comes to a common agreement about something (in our case, the validity of a transaction) without having to trust one another. This is also known as distributed trust-less consensus and is a major research topic in the field of Distributed Systems. Many algorithms have been designed to solve this problem of distributed consensus. Cryptocurrencies like Bitcoin use a specific protocol called *Proof of Work* (POW), as we've seen, which lets the blockchain network achieve distributed consensus and operate without getting tampered with. It is important to understand why achieving distributed consensus is so important in a cryptocurrency's blockchain network.

Let's assume that you have a network of computers (or "nodes") that are interconnected in a haphazard manner. This network forms the *backend* of your service. In other words, all the computation and database storage operations are handled by this network *behind the scenes*. Your objective is to ensure that when a user performs an action, it has to be recorded and updated congruently throughout the network. So your network is distributed but you have to project a single consistent experience to users everywhere. This is the most basic requirement for not only a cryptocurrency like bitcoin but also for almost every technology company out there like Google, Facebook, Amazon, Instagram etc.

When a user performs an action, you will observe that in order to achieve the objective of consistency, you are inevitably left with only two options. Either record this action in all the nodes or none of the nodes. If you record it in only some of the nodes, there is an inconsistency in the network and the nodes cannot figure out the truth i.e, whether the user did actually perform the action or not. In other words, the network cannot come to an agreeable consensus. This is a big problem because an inconsistent network is an insecure network. Any hacker would be able to exploit this inconsistency to spread viruses or manipulate the database to his/her advantage. Therefore, it is important for a distributed network to maintain consistent data across all nodes and be able to identify erroneous and inconsistent records quickly. This is the reason why distributed consensus is so important in a blockchain network.

Now let's look at how exactly the blockchain aids in achieving this decentralized consensus. We will be considering bitcoin as the reference cryptocurrency.

Decentralized consensus in a blockchain is truly amazing. This is because all the nodes in the network are able to agree on the validity of a transaction without having to trust anyone else or knowing the identity of parties involved. That is why it is also known as trust-less decentralized consensus.

Decentralized consensus in a cryptocurrency using blockchain is achieved in an emergent manner. What this means is that there is no single point of time at which all the nodes in the network are able to agree on the validity of a transaction. As time progresses, more and more nodes will be able to arrive at the same conclusion.

There are four phases in which this emergent distributed consensus is achieved. Let's look at them closely.

**Phase #1: Verification of every incoming transaction by every node.**

The nodes in the network receive data regarding various transactions from their neighboring nodes. Some of these transactions are just invalid. So, as a primary rule, all the nodes check the incoming transactions and collect the valid ones into what is called as a *transaction pool* or *mempool*. The transactions are verified using cryptographic techniques based on a list of criteria that are public.

And this pool of valid but unconfirmed transactions are propagated across the network by each node. So all the invalid transactions are weeded out by the nodes in the network.

**Phase #2: Mining nodes accumulate valid transactions into blocks.**

Mining nodes, as we've seen earlier, are special nodes in the network whose job is to collect valid transactions from their neighboring nodes, put them in a block and compute a unique value (*"Proof of Work"*) for the block using a cryptographic algorithm. The mining nodes keep track of the latest blocks and compete with each other to create a new block of these valid transactions with the appropriate *proof-of-work*. These blocks are then propagated across the network to other nodes.

**Phase #3: Nodes receive and verify blocks**

As the nodes in the network receive blocks from various mining nodes, they calculate their validity. Anybody can accumulate transactions into blocks. But the trick here is that computing the correct *"proof-of-work"* of a block is very hard and therefore reduces the chance of a transaction fraud. Once the nodes receive a mining node's block, they verify it against the *"proof-of-work"* and add it to their *blockchain* which they've been maintaining and updating so far.

**Phase #4: Nodes eliminate irrelevant blocks**

Every node maintains and updates its own blockchain which is essentially a list of blocks that are considered valid using publicly known and accepted criteria. Nodes can receive multiple valid blocks by different mining nodes. So how can they decide collectively as to which of the received blocks should be considered while extending the blockchain? This is where the proof-of-work protocol comes in handy. Different blocks have different proof-of-work values. The bitcoin protocol states that while selecting blocks, preference should be given to those with highest proof-of-work value. So if a node gets two different blocks, it will maintain two separate lists in the blockchain until one of them exceeds the other in the total cumulative proof-of-work value sum. It will then discard the sub-chain with lower proof-of-work value sum. In a way, the nodes give preference to the sub-chain in which the mining nodes have spent more computational power because the *proof-of-work* value sum is a measure of the amount of computation done by the mining nodes.

**The Double-Spending Problem**

The concept of blockchain was first brought to light by the Bitcoin inventor, Satoshi Nakamoto. It was(and still is) considered a brilliant engineering design partly because it was able to solve what no other digital currency could, before that point of time, which is to *'Ensure that the cryptocurrency units cannot be spent more than once.'* This is termed as the double spending problem.

Unlike fiat currency, the problem with a virtual currency is not the creation of the currency units. Anybody can come up with protocols/algorithms defining how the virtual currency units need to be created, how they need to be structured, what the size (in bytes) of each unit should be and so on. But the fundamental problem that any currency, especially a digital currency, needs to solve is *Double Spending*.

A *double-spend* is a scenario in which one unit of currency is spent in two separate transactions. This can be done by duplicating the unit itself or manipulating the record of transactions. In case of cryptocurrencies, this 'record' is the blockchain ledger. A typical fiat currency solves the double-spending problem by deploying special techniques to print the cash and identify fake bills. The banks that deal with fiat currency transactions also take extensive security measures to prevent their databases (which hold all the transaction and account details) from getting hacked and hijacked. If the security of the bank's computer-network was compromised, the potential for damage is huge. With countless cases of bank frauds, hacking attacks and duplication of cash, it is evident that a fiat currency's solution to the double-spending problem is undoubtedly flawed.

**So, how does a cryptocurrency like bitcoin solve this?**
Unlike a centralized fiat currency, a system like bitcoin does not maintain "balances" of the individuals. It only maintains a ledger of transactions a.k.a the blockchain. So the only way to handle this issue is by assigning identifiers to bitcoins so that

when someone tries to spend a bitcoin with the same identifier twice, it can be checked against the transactions recorded in the blockchain.

The way this works is, whenever you send someone bitcoins, that transaction is identified and recorded using a UTXO which is short for Unspent Transaction Output. This UTXO is the unique identifier that represents a transaction of bitcoins which is similar to a bill of fiat currency. UTXOs can be spent only as wholes. But they can be converted into multiple smaller UTXOs for transaction convenience.

When you want to spend some bitcoins, you have to either merge or split two UTXOs to create the new set of UTXOs you want. For example, consider that you have two UTXOs of 0.3 and 0.6 bitcoins, received from Alice and Bob respectively. Let's refer to these using their IDs, X and Y. So X represents the UTXO of Alice and Y that of Bob. And let's say that you want to send 0.7 bitcoins to Carter. The conversion goes as follows:

X(0.3 bitcoins) + Y(0.6 bitcoins) => Z(0.7 bitcoins) + W(0.2 bitcoins)

Z and W represent the unique IDs of two new UTXOs created so that 0.7 bitcoins can be sent to Carter. Now, this new UTXO(Z) can only be spent when used in conjunction with Carter's signature. It is propagated across the network and eventually picked up by a mining node which hashes it into a block and updates the blockchain. That is how the transaction takes place. And the conversion is handled by a software called the *cryptocurrency wallet* which we'll be looking into later in this chapter. The other UTXO(W) worth 0.2 bitcoins goes back into your wallet and is spendable only in conjunction with your signature.

With this framework in place, all that a node has to do to verify if a bitcoin is being "double-spent" is to check the UTXO ID against the blockchain's transactions. Even if a node's blockchain is incomplete, the faulty UTXO will get propagated only so far before getting dropped by the other nodes with complete blockchain which can verify transactions.

## Who maintains the servers and Why?

You must be wondering, if maintaining and updating the blockchain takes so much effort, who would want to do this? Why would anyone want to volunteer for this kind of a thing?

The answer to that is *mining incentives.* As we've already seen, most cryptocurrencies are designed in such a way that the people who validate transactions and update the blockchain are rewarded with new crypto-coins. This serves them as an incentive for their efforts. Rewarding the miners is the only sustainable way of maintaining a distributed decentralized cryptocurrency network. This is because mining the crypto-coins requires a lot of computational power provided by specialized GPUs and also involves paying a lot of money in electricity bill.

It also happens to be that mining is the only way of generating cryptocurrency i.e, the new crypto-coins in the network are only generated when a miner creates a new valid block. This is a clever strategy to solve two problems in one shot. The miners get incentivized and the network gets new crypto-coins to work with.

It is very important for the system to be designed in such a way that **anybody** can come in and volunteer as a miner in the network. If the ability to mine was exclusive, the banks or the government or the top 1% could find a way to attain too much control over the system. This could jeopardize the safety and decentralization of the cryptocurrency. For example, if a bank was bombed and/or its servers were hacked, its customers would be in trouble. But with a widespread network of mining volunteers, there wouldn't be a single point of failure. This was something that Satoshi Nakomoto made sure of, while designing the system framework.

**Why is it safe?**

For the purpose of answering this question, let's narrow our focus down to one single cryptocurrency – bitcoin. Bitcoin is the most widely used cryptocurrency in the world. Millions of people pay close attention to the bitcoin network every day. The software itself undergoes regular public updates **(https://github.com/bitcoin/bitcoin)**. A 2013 article on Forbes suggests that the global bitcoin computing power is 256 times more than the top 500 supercomputers in the world. That should give you a measure of the number of servers being run by the bitcoin volunteers. So at this point of time, the only possible ways to hack bitcoin are by taking down the internet or cracking the SHA256 function. This of course, is regarding the overall bitcoin network and the system design. You can still get your bitcoins lost/stolen if you do not follow the recommended security measures (described later in the chapter) while operating your wallet.

Having said that, let's look at the probability of someone cracking the SHA256.

As we've learned in chapter-2, SHA256 is a cryptographic hash function. By definition, that means that the similarity between two outputs for two similar inputs is very low. In the context of a cryptocurrency, we can say that SHA256 is cracked when a hacker can take a block of transactions, modify it somehow and end up with the same hash output of 256 bits as the original block. This way, when the nodes try to verify the hash value of the modified block, they will be unable to identify the hack.

Now let's look at exactly how a hacker can go about pulling this off. Let's represent the original block as OB, original hash value as OH and the modified block as MB.

The problem that the hacker needs to solve is to find a MB such that: SHA256 (MB) = OH.

We know that OH has 256 bits. We know that a bit can have two possible values (1 or 0). This means that there are $2^{256}$ possible values for the output of SHA256 function. But since SHA256 is not just any function but specifically a cryptographic hash function (random outputs for two similar inputs), the only way to generate a desired output is to iterate over all possible inputs and somehow end up with the same output hash as OH. And since OH has 256 bits, the hacker has to, on average, iterate over at least $2^{256}$ inputs to find a possible match. Now let's appreciate the difficulty associated with this task. There is a video by the YouTube creator 3blue1brown (http://www.3blue1brown.com) that explains this very creatively. It's a really good animated video and I would recommend you to check it out. Here's the gist of it:

$2^{256}$ is $2^{32}$ multiplied by itself 8 times.

So $2^{256} = 2^{32} * 2^{32} * 2^{32} * 2^{32} * 2^{32} * 2^{32} * 2^{32} * 2^{32}$

The value of $2^{32}$ is around 4 billion.

So consider the following approximation.

$2^{256}$ = (4billion) * (4billion) *(4billion) *(4billion) *(4billion) *(4billion) *(4billion) *(4billion)

A good GPU can do less than 1 billion hashes per second. Suppose you create a specialized computer/server that uses 4 of these GPUs to perform 4 billion hashes per second. This takes care of the first 4billion factor of $2^{256}$. Now assume you can somehow get a hold of 4billion of these specialized computers. To put things in perspective, reports say that Google, which is the biggest search engine and probably the most-used website on the internet, has only around 900,000 servers in its data centers. 4 billion is 4000 times a million. So assuming you can somehow get hold of 4000 times the number of computers that Google has, you will be able to take care of the first two factors of $2^{256}$. That still leaves out 6 more factors. To take care of another 4billion factor, assume everyone on earth gets a hold of their personal sever-farm of 4billion specialized hash computers. There are around 7.442 billion people on earth so that takes care of the third factor.

We still have 5 more factors to go. How do we handle those? Let's assume you communicate with aliens and somehow get access to 4billion planets hosting 4billion aliens each of whom has 4billion specialized computers. That takes care of the 4$^{th}$ factor. We're half way through. Only 4 more to go. Now imagine 4 billion galaxies each of which has such 4billion planets. That leaves out just 3 more factors. We've tried scaling with computational resources. Now let's try to scale with time. 4 billion seconds is around 126.8 years. 4 billion times that is 507 billion years which is estimated to be 37 times the age of the universe itself. Even with that, we still have one more factor left.

So the bottom line is this: If everyone on earth was using 4billion specialized computers and there were 4billion such earths in a galaxy and 4billion of such galaxies, it would take them 37 times the age of the universe to calculate $1/2^{32}$ of the total possibilities of $2^{256}$. I don't know about you but that seems pretty unreal to me. So yes I'd bet on the security of SHA-256.

Now that we know how hard it is to crack SHA256, it is important to understand the difference between safety and anonymity in the context of cryptocurrencies. The fact that SHA256 is hard to crack only implies that an attack on the blockchain or stealing your crypto-coins is extremely unlikely. It, however, does not mean that you are anonymous within the system. This is one of the biggest misconceptions about bitcoin and other cryptocurrencies. Your bitcoins are safe but your identity is not a total secret.

Most cryptocurrencies including Bitcoin only provide pseudonymity and not complete anonymity. Although your identity is not revealed openly, the transaction details are updated on the blockchain which is accessible by anyone. Using techniques like cluster analysis and pattern recognition on the data from the public blockchain, one can start to form associations with your activity and your IP-address (which is essentially your online identity). Now, you can use software like Tor or VPN to hide your IP address but the fact of the matter is that even Tor cannot guarantee complete anonymity. A dedicated hacker with enough resources can eventually track your IP address down. But, he/she will not be able to steal or tamper with your crypto-coins. Having said that, if you're still concerned, I would recommend that you choose Zcash as it is the most pseudonymous cryptocurrency out there. To make it more convenient for the cryptocurrency users to transact safely, a complementary software called the *wallet* is used to ensure higher privacy. Let's look at how that works.

**Cryptocurrency wallet**

A cryptocurrency wallet, or *crypto-wallet* for short, is a digital holder for your cryptocurrency (like bitcoin) and is mandatory for performing transactions. It stores your private, public keys and manages your cryptocurrency transactions by interacting with the blockchain. There is no such thing as a bitcoin without a wallet identification. Every cryptocurrency unit has to be associated with, and transacted using, a wallet. You cannot spend your crypto-coins without the wallet. You also cannot spend the same crypto-coins from multiple wallets because it doesn't tally with the blockchain's record.

There are different types of wallets you can use. You will find below, an image of a mobile wallet which is essentially a mobile app that stores your public & private key data and manages your transactions. The specific screenshot has been taken from the "Bitcoin Wallet" app on Google Play Store. There are other types of wallet frameworks like desktop wallet application, online wallet (website), hardware wallet (USB drive, hard disk etc), paper wallet (printed sheet of keys in a QR code).

**How does the wallet work?**

A crypto-wallet holds 3 primary values. The public key, private key and the amount of crypto-coins. As we've seen, the primary purpose of a wallet is to facilitate cryptocurrency transactions.

*Here's how it does it.*

Let's say that you want to send bitcoins to your friend. Your wallet will generate the transaction-message, amount of bitcoins you want to send and sign (encrypt) it with your private key and your friend's public key. This message is then communicated over an online network channel with your friend. Your friend's wallet will verify if the message is in fact sent by you and intended for him by decrypting it with his private key and your public key.

After the authenticity is established and the possibility of a middle-man is eliminated, your friend's wallet increases the amount of bitcoins it holds and sends a response. Once your wallet receives the response, it decreases your bitcoin amount.

There is a specific Wallet protocol put in place to ensure that the amounts in the two wallets corresponding to a transaction are modified correctly. Anybody who wishes to implement their own wallet software must adhere to this protocol or else the transactions won't be processed. For more details, check out the following link. **https://en.bitcoin.it/wiki/Wallet_protocol**

After the amounts in both the wallets are modified, the blockchain is updated with the transaction entry. It takes some time for the blockchain network to validate the transaction. If all goes well, the ledger moves forward otherwise the error in the system will notify the wallets and the change is reverted. This concludes a typical wallet use-case scenario.

For the purpose of simplicity, many details have been omitted. If you're looking for more specifics, please visit the official bitcoin developer guide on this topic at: **https://bitcoin.org/en/developer-guide#wallets**

**Security Measures for Cryptocurrency Wallets**

Losing the wallet or the keys will result in **\*TOTAL LOSS\*** of your cryptocurrency. It might helpful to learn about a famous real-life story of James Howells who lost 7500 bitcoins (worth $19.6 million today) because he accidentally threw his old hard drive into the trash bin while clearing his desk. That hard drive is now reportedly buried under four feet of junk in a landfill site in Newport.

So make no mistake, the security of your wallet should be your top most priority when dealing with cryptocurrency.

Here are some tips to follow.

**Tip #1**: There are different wallet softwares you can choose for any cryptocurrency. Please use only an officially recognized wallet to avoid issues of security and malfunction. Take some time and go through the wallet specifications and your cryptocurrency's website to pick what's best. For bitcoin, you can find all the recommended bitcoin wallets at: **https://bitcoin.org/en/choose-your-wallet**.

**Tip #2**: Encrypt your wallet and private key and have multiple copies stored in secure locations (online and offline). Make sure that you have at least one copy available in an accessible physical device like a flash drive or a hard disk.

**Tip #3**: If the amount of your cryptocurrency is substantial, it is recommended to use multiple wallets to distribute the possible damage that can happen. Use 2-step verification methods or MultiSig (Multiple Signature) transactions.

# Chapter 4

## Investing in Cryptocurrencies

*Tips to follow and pitfalls to avoid*

If all the recent news and public attention to cryptocurrencies has piqued your interest in the subject and you would like to test the market out for yourself, this chapter is for you. Even if you don't already own a brokerage account, you will find that the process of investing in and trading with cryptocurrencies is actually quite simple.

**The process**

Decide which cryptocurrency you want to invest in. You can take a look at all the available ones, including their price and market capitalization at CoinMarketCap (www.coinmarketcap.com) or CoinCap (www.coincap.io). The most popular cryptocurrencies currently are Bitcoin, Ethereum and Ripple.

After selecting a cryptocurrency, you need to pick an Exchange to operate with. An exchange is basically a market platform through which you can buy or sell publicly traded items (shares/equities). Just like regular company stocks which have exchanges like NASDAQ or NYSE, cryptocurrencies have their own exchanges which can be found at CryptoCoinCharts (www.cryptocoincharts.info/markets/info). Please note that it's not necessary for an exchange to support all cryptocurrencies. And some of them might not be supported in your geographical area. So browse through the exchanges carefully and select one that you find suitable. Here are some parameters to judge the exchange on: reputation and public opinion, supported payment options, transaction fee, geographical limitations, supported cryptocurrencies, ease of usage. The most popular exchanges are CoinBase and Kraken. I personally use CoinBase because it satisfies all the criteria for me. And so far, it has been a safe and smooth ride without any issue. Use the link below to sign up and get $10 bonus for your first trade.

https://www.coinbase.com/join/598b36cb68284c0125fa0aea

After picking a suitable exchange, you will need to verify your identity (passport, driver's license etc) to create an account. Once the account is created, you will be able to add/withdraw funds and start trading. Just like any other trading platform, you will be charged a very small fee for every trade to keep the exchange going.

You might be wondering as to why your ID is required when after all, cryptocurrencies are supposed to be decentralized and supportive of users' privacy/anonymity preferences. Well, here's the thing. Although the transactions themselves are private, the cryptocurrency exchange needs initial fiat currency funds to assign you crypto-coins to trade with. And where there is fiat currency involved, there is a non-zero probability of financial fraud. So, to avoid issues with unoriginal fiat currency (stolen credit cards etc), the exchange does require your personal information to validate your fiat money. Once you've been verified, you can trade on the platform with privacy.

**Pitfalls to avoid**

Given the volatility of the market in the recent times, it helps to be aware of the obvious and not-so-obvious mistakes before making your investments. Here are some points to keep in mind so that you don't become the next 'riches to rags' story.

- One thing you have to be aware of, more than anything else, is that you cannot reverse a cryptocurrency transaction through the exchange i.e, cancellation and refund are not available as options. So before you trade your crypto-coins, double check to make sure everything is accurate.

- Only invest in cryptocurrencies that have a good reputation and/or credibility. You don't want people to run away with your money. So do your homework well and invest in projects that you feel like you can trust or that have a proven track record. Stay away from the seemingly fake cryptocurrencies which just have a good-looking website but no solid team or vision behind it.

- Do not store too much cryptocurrency in the exchange. Make sure to transfer the traded crypto-coins back to your wallet safely. This is because, you want to ensure that your crypto-coins are secure even if the exchange gets hacked. Mt.Gox which was the largest bitcoin exchange at one point, got hacked and filed for bankruptcy. So there's no long-term guarantee of safety if you hold your money on the exchange itself.

- While transferring your cryptocurrency from the exchange to the wallet (and vice versa), pay very close attention and only use the public key in your wallet. Never reveal or share your private key in a public context. **Even if the exchange asks you for it.**


**Tips and Strategies**

<u>Tip #1</u>: Figure out exactly how much you want to invest before you get your feet wet. If you're a beginner, make sure that this amount is not greater than 5-10% of your total financial assets. You should only invest your extra savings. And be prepared to lose this initial amount as your primary goal early on would be to experiment with different strategies and test the market. Also, it's advised to begin with bitcoin and ethereum if you're a

beginner crypto-trader. Once you get an understanding of how it all works, you can chip in with higher amounts and try other cryptocurrencies or ICOs (we'll look into this in a short while). But you must always acknowledge the risks involved and be prepared for the worst possible outcome.

**Tip #2**: Make sure to understand the ins and outs of the cryptocurrency before investing. Hopefully by reading this book, you have acquired a basic knowledge of the cryptocurrency landscape. For more details, you may want to dig further into the technology to get a better sense of what and where you're putting your money. You can read the latest news, reviews, design documents etc. If you're a programmer, you can read the code which is open-sourced so it's viewable by the public. If you're not a programmer and want to get more perspective, I wrote a separate book called *"Bitcoin: The Digital Gold"* which I'd recommend to anyone interested in buying or investing in bitcoin. It is a deeper and more focused look at the Bitcoin network with clear explanations.

**Tip #3**: Don't be impatient. Never buy/sell because of the hype. When markets fluctuate drastically, people usually fall victim to a phenomenon called *FOMO* (Fear of Missing Out). This is when you start selling frantically as the value drops and start buying madly as the value rises. Despite the general philosophy being *buy low sell high*, it is always advantageous to think clearly and anticipate the hype instead of falling for it. Impatience is probably the #1 way that people lose money trading online. A guy I know bought 10 bitcoins back in 2015 for around $231 and sold them when the price reached $455. He was ecstatic because of the $2240 profit he made. But if he had not fallen for the quick profit and stuck with the bitcoins, he would've made $32,000 as of yesterday's evaluation.

**Tip #4**: Don't spend all your earnings away. Despite being so simple, this is something newbie investors and traders fail at, very often. They make a quick buck and go spend it on luxury items to feel good. That's a fundamentally flawed approach when dealing with long-term asset building. You have to save your earnings and either invest them on building your skills/knowledge or use it as capital for making your next trade.

Now let's look at some of the strategies you can use to actually make profits by trading or investing in cryptocurrencies.

**Strategy #1**: ICOs

Split your amount into 10 equal parts and invest them into 10 different ICOs. An ICO (Initial Coin Offering) is similar to crowdfunding where you can invest in a startup by purchasing cryptocurrency. However, unlike true crowdfunding, the investors' prime interest is to get back profits and not necessarily to donate to the startup. The startup will use this investment as capital to work on its project(s) and if it's successful, the value of the cryptocurrency will raise substantially. An example of a good ICO is the Ethereum project which raised money initially at $0.4 per ether which is currently valued at $203 with a market cap of over $19 billion. So when you invest in 10 ICOs, the likelihood of winning at least one of those bets is reasonably high. The win rate, as described by the cryptocurrency experts, is usually around 20%. This means that 2 out of your 10 ICO investments have a good chance of giving you 10X or more returns. Even if you already have some bitcoins, you can invest them in other cryptocurrencies with high potential (during ICOs) to make a profit.

**Strategy #2**: Disruptive cryptocurrencies

Once you pass the beginner phase of investing in cryptocurrencies, you will start to look for long-term profits. One way to increase your probability of getting these is to do your research and identify the cryptocurrencies which are inherently disruptive. For example, Bitcoin was the first of its kind to offer a proper decentralized digital currency. Similarly, Ethereum's smart contracts are disrupting the legal side of business. So if you read the white papers and do some proper research, you will eventually be able to identify those **\*disruptive cryptocurrencies\*** and that's where you'll have a higher chance of making long-term profits.

**Strategy #3**: Short when the price is low

"Shorting" is basically betting against the market. It's not as rebellious/risky as it sounds (when done properly of course). Traditionally, profits in trading happen by buying low and selling high. This is when buying happens before selling. What if you could sell first and then buy later? That's how shorting works. You basically borrow bitcoin/Altcoins initially and sell it first when the value is relatively high. And then, you observe the market to see when the value drops. As soon as it does, you buy back the cryptocurrency you've sold and this leads to a profit. The amount you've borrowed to sell the coins initially is automatically returned back by the software you use. Shorting cryptocurrencies is much less riskier than shorting traditional stocks in a stock exchange. To observe the value-change of the cryptocurrencies in real time, you can use CoinCap (www.coincap.io). Note that shorting works better with short-term dips but not with long-term growths.

**Is it all just a big bubble?**
Many people ask this question when they see the market prices plunge up/down. One of the biggest arguments people make in this regard is, "Well, if it's decentralized, who's gonna back it up?" There is no authority backing up the system. So it is easy to fall into the trap of thinking that cryptocurrencies are just

treading on thin ice and have no solid ground to stand on. But this couldn't be farther from the fact. What gives, say, Bitcoin, its value is its huge user base and widespread acceptance. If you think about it, that's what gives anything value. Public acceptance. Not centralized government backing. If you take a commodity like an Apple iPhone and ask the question "Why is it worth what it's worth?" the answer will be the same. IPhones are not backed by the government the way fiat currencies are. They are just a company's products that people have come to assign great value to, over time due to various factors. So cryptocurrencies get their value the same way an iPhone gets its value. Public acceptance. The more they're used by the people, the more they're worth. And as far as reliability goes, I think Bitcoin's current market capitalization of over $52billion speaks for itself.

With cryptocurrencies, it is almost certain at this point that the total market cap will reach $1Trillion within the next 5 years. We are currently at a total of around $111Billion. With the amount of progress being made in this field, even with a temporary value-drop or a bubble-pop, the rise of cryptocurrencies and blockchain technology is inevitable. So brace yourselves for what is to come. Having said that, if you follow some of the common-sense tips mentioned in this chapter, diversify your capital and use common sense, you will have a smoother sailing.

# Chapter 5

## Future of Cryptocurrency

*Where are we headed?*

At the time of this writing (July 2017), cryptocurrencies have a smaller user base compared to fiat currencies. But as technology improves and more infrastructure and awareness are created around the world, the impact of cryptocurrencies is inevitable and immense.

Venture Capitalists have invested more than 1 Billion dollars into the blockchain technology itself. This is an indication of the scope of development that is bound to occur in this field in the upcoming future. Below is a graph showing the increase in number of user-wallets of bitcoin's blockchain.

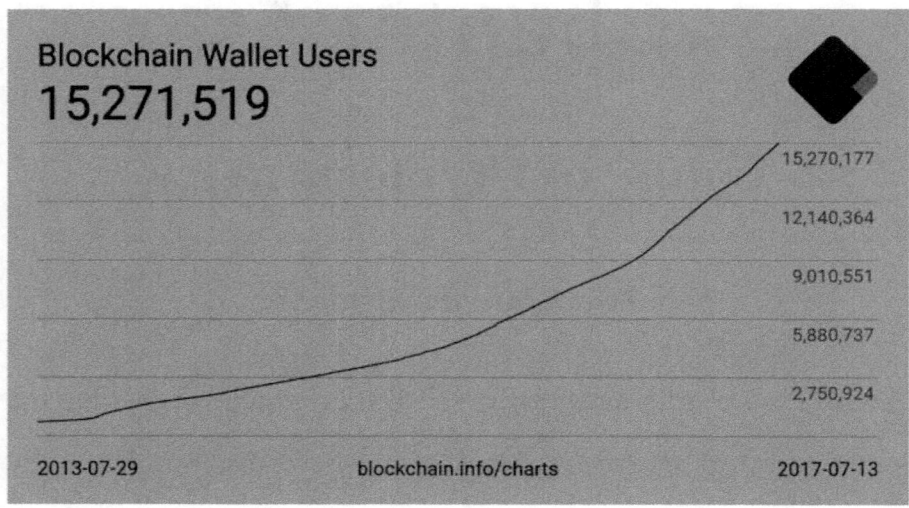

There are more and more cryptocurrencies coming into the market every month. As time goes on, we will see a range of cryptocurrencies offering different services for users. Bitcoin being the first one out there, will have an initial head start in terms of user adoption. But with all the latest innovations and the attention being paid to this space, it is difficult to predict whether bitcoin will be overtaken by other cryptocurrencies or not. As shown below in the graph from *CoinMarketCap*, Bitcoin currently occupies more than 51% of the total market share of cryptocurrencies.

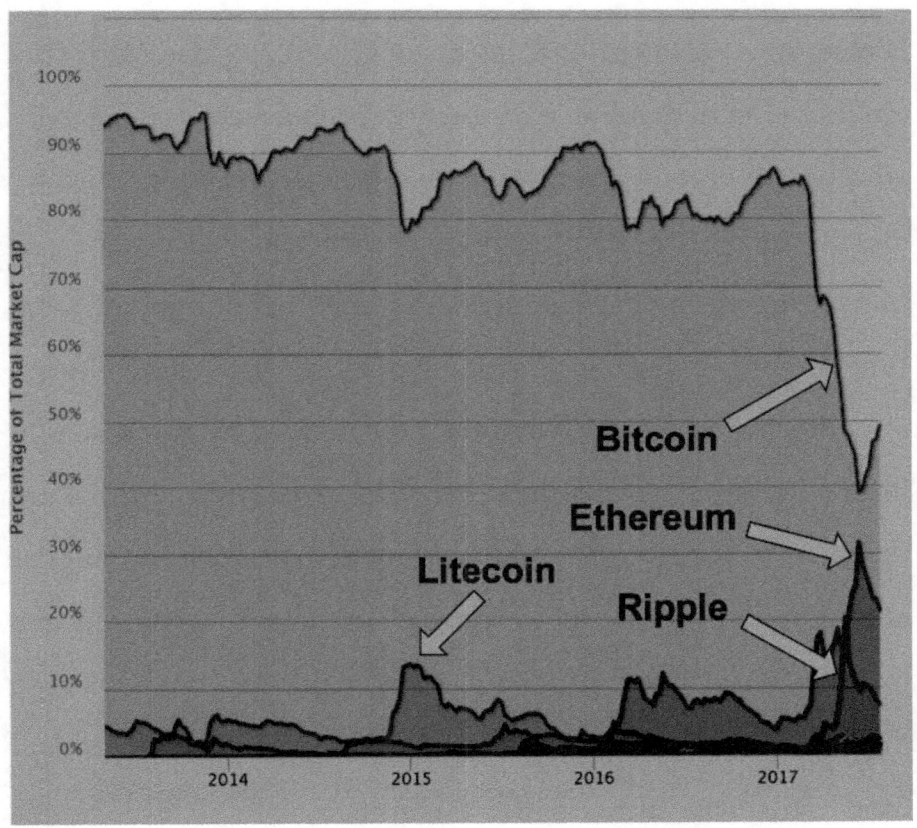

The advent of these new cryptocurrencies will be paralleled by an emergence of new crypto-exchanges. So it will get easier for merchants and buyers to transfer the money and convert between two cryptocurrencies.

Having said this, I think we need to look at both sides of the coin (no pun intended). One of the biggest problems facing the mass adoption of cryptocurrencies is their lack of scalability. Bitcoin, for example, has had a huge growth in the number of transactions being carried out. The graph below, sourced from Wikipedia, shows how the number of transactions has been growing every year. But here's the catch – The block-size in Bitcoin is limited to 1MB. So any blocks bigger than this are rejected by the network. This has resulted in limiting the number of transactions per second that can be processed by the network to three. To counter this limit, bitcoin miners have opted to upgrade the software so that the block-size can be increased to 2MB. This will increase the transaction fee but reduce the congestion in the network.

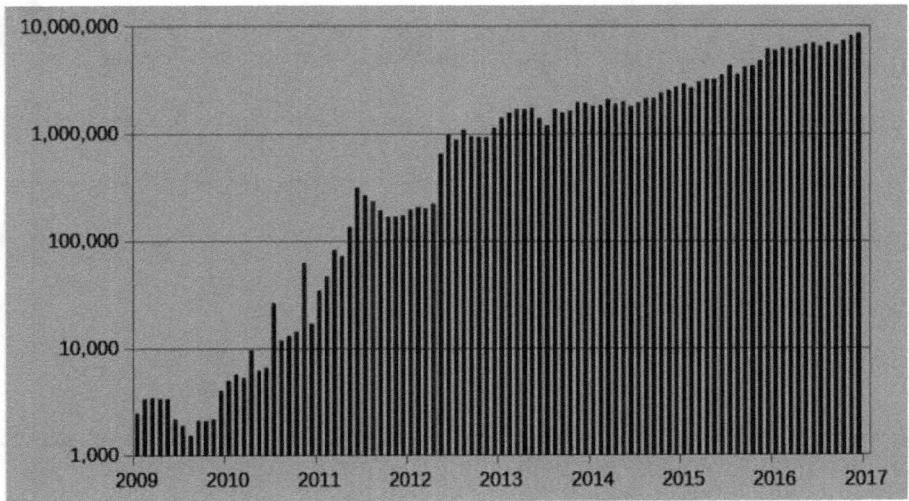

Bitcoin also had a bear market crash recently (July 2017) where it's value dropped by around 20% in a 7-day period. Although the value is back up again, it would be foolish to believe that the cryptocurrency market is not volatile. It is highly advised for anyone interested in investing into cryptocurrencies or anyone that has already done so, to follow the latest updates and stay informed.

**The Changing Landscape of Global Finance**

With features like lower latency of transactions and reduced transaction fee, cryptocurrencies (especially bitcoin) have a potential for disrupting the e-commerce industry as well. The current online payment methods that users have to rely on for purchasing stuff online have lousy user experience, charge more per transaction and take longer to process payments. This gives cryptocurrencies like Bitcoin an opportunity to replace the traditional methods and create positive impact.

Due to its decentralized nature, Bitcoin has been facing restricted compliance from the banks and financial organizations. Its value dropped quite a bit when China banned Bitcoin from being used within its borders. But with blockchain, it's a different story. Financial institutions are showing positive response to the possibility of embracing the public ledger system. The reason for this seems to be the increase in operational efficiency created by using the blockchain technology.

Cryptocurrencies also seem to be advantageous for third-world countries that have under-developed financial infrastructure. These countries can bypass the need for spending a lot of tax money into public banks, mints and other regulatory financial organizations by directly adopting global cryptocurrencies like

Bitcoin. What we're looking at is actually the possibility of unifying the world's currencies.

There are a lot of experiments being conducted in this space and despite all the hype, cryptocurrencies are still in their early stages. So there is absolutely no need for you to feel like you're missing out on the party. Cryptocurrencies and blockchain have the potential to change not only the payment industry but also the way business is done. With widespread decentralized distributed digital currencies, there would be no need for separate national fiat currencies. All countries around the world could fall back on a single platform of value exchange. If it happens, this will be a landmark achievement in the history of human progress. Although we have a long way to go before achieving that stage, it is quite obvious that the future of cryptocurrencies is very bright indeed.

# Chapter 6

## Conclusion

You've made it! I would like to personally congratulate you for reading through the book all the way to the end. Let's not underestimate the rarity and importance of this action. Research shows that 57% of total books in U.S are not read till completion. So that statistic alone should make you pat yourself on the back. Good job!

We have covered many topics in the preceding chapters. From the origin of money to the future of cryptocurrencies, we've gone through all the essential motions. If some of it felt overwhelming, don't worry. Without a technology background, it's understandably hard to wrap your head around some of the deeper concepts. A professor of mine once said that consuming knowledge is like consuming food. You don't try to swallow it whole. You should chop down the food into small pieces and take your time to consume them one by one. That's the way it goes with books too. Going by that metaphor, I hope you had your tummy full after reading this book. In case you haven't, here's a quick recap of the fundamentals. A little brush up will help you store the information you've learned to sink in deeper into your memory.

- Money is a representation of value as recognized by the entities participating in the value-exchange.
- Currency is the set of all units of money which are in use at any given point of time.
- Money is abstract while currency is real and tangible.
- Fiat currency consists of the notes and coins authorized and distributed by the government.
- Cryptocurrency is one form of digital currency where cryptography is used to create and safe keep the money.
- There are more than 900 cryptocurrencies currently available and more are bound to enter the market soon.
- There are many advantages of using a cryptocurrency. Durability, Divisibility, Privacy are some of them.
- Bitcoin was the first cryptocurrency to get widespread public attention and acceptance. It was created as a result of works

by an anonymous identity called Satoshi Nakomoto.
- The core technology behind most of the cryptocurrencies is a public-ledger system called the blockchain.
- The Blockchain is an open record of valid transactions made using the cryptocurrency. It is a protection against frauds and counterfeits.
- Special nodes in the network, called miners, update the blockchain by validating blocks of transactions. For this, they are compensated with a reward of some amount of crypto-coins. These rewards are the only way the system generates new cryptocurrency i.e, by incentivizing computations.
- Anybody can volunteer for running a mining node. This is how the network aims to remain decentralized.
- The two main problems that the blockchain solves are: achieving decentralized consensus and solving double spending.
- Decentralized consensus is a state in which all the nodes in a cryptocurrency network can agree on something (like validity of a transaction). In Bitcoin, it is achieved with the help of a protocol called *Proof-of-Work*.

- Double spending is a situation in which a user tries to spend the same unit in two separate transactions. It is solved using UTXOs (Unspent Transaction Outputs) to represent the transactions instead of managing user-balances.
- The underlying security framework used to keep cryptocurrencies safe is called SHA256. It is a cryptographic function that converts input data into outputs of size 256-bits. It is considered impossible to crack.
- You should be extra careful while using your crypto-wallets to store and transfer cryptocurrency. Never reveal your private key to others. Backup your wallet and store your cryptocurrency in multiple chunks instead of one single location.
- You can purchase and trade cryptocurrencies at a cryptocurrency exchange. Recommended exchanges are *CoinBase* and *Kraken*.
- *CoinMarketCap* is a good place to follow up on the trends of different cryptocurrencies. For useful tips and strategies, make sure that you're subscribed to my list at : **www.bit.ly/devan-hansel**

- While investing in cryptocurrencies, double-check to make sure they're safe and have a proven track record. Once made, reversing the transactions isn't easy. Also don't store your crypto-coins on the exchange for too long. Get them back on to your wallet as quickly as possible.
- ICOs(Initial Coin Offerings) are great opportunities to invest in budding startups that need capital to finish their projects. A good ICO can give 10-30X returns on your investment.
- A lot of money, time and effort is going into the cryptocurrency market. The right time to get started is Now!

# A humble request

Hey reader! I would like to, once again, express my gratitude to you for buying and reading this book. I hope you found some value for your time. But before we part our ways, I'd really appreciate it if you could just do this ONE thing to help me out.

Please leave a review on Amazon.

As a principle, I have always steered towards giving as much value as I can without any expectation. Not to sound too deep but I've found that service is what brings meaning into my life personally. I've done my best to write a good and useful book. But there are many people out there that can benefit from the information provided here. To help me serve better, I request you to leave an honest review. That will help me learn and also reach out to others. Thanks a ton!

# More books from the author

**Bitcoin**: The Digital Gold

**Blockchain**: The Technology Revolution behind Bitcoin and Cryptocurrency

www.ingramcontent.com/pod-product-compliance
Lightning Source LLC
Chambersburg PA
CBHW070312230526
45470CB00002B/840